Mad Anthony Wayne: The Life and Legacy of the Famous Revolutionary War General

By Charles River Editors

About Charles River Editors

Charles River Editors is a boutique digital publishing company, specializing in bringing history back to life with educational and engaging books on a wide range of topics. Keep up to date with our new and free offerings with this 5 second sign up on our weekly mailing list, and visit Our Kindle Author Page to see other recently published Kindle titles.

We make these books for you and always want to know our readers' opinions, so we encourage you to leave reviews and look forward to publishing new and exciting titles each week.

Introduction

"Issue the orders Sir, and I will storm Hell." – Mad Anthony Wayne

The American Revolution is replete with seminal moments that every American learns in school, from the "shot heard 'round the world" to the Declaration of Independence, but the events that led up to the fighting at Lexington & Concord were borne out of 10 years of division between the British and their American colonies over everything from colonial representation in governments to taxation, the nature of searches, and the quartering of British regulars in private houses. From 1764-1775, a chain of events that included lightning rods like the Townshend Acts led to bloodshed in the form of the Boston Massacre, while the Boston Tea Party became a symbol of nonviolent protest.

The political and military nature of the Revolutionary War was just as full of intrigue. While disorganized militias fought the Battles of Lexington & Concord, George Washington would lead the Continental Army in the field while men like Thomas Jefferson drafted the Declaration of Independence in Philadelphia and Benjamin Franklin negotiated overseas in France. Benedict Arnold would become one of his nation's most vital war heroes and its most notorious traitor, French forces would play a crucial role at the end of the war, and the Treaty of Paris would conclude the Revolution with one last great surprise.

One of the most unique aspects of the Revolutionary War is that a number of the most recognizable American heroes of that war hailed from overseas. When the Revolution began, the Continental Army sported numerous volunteers from Ireland, Scotland, virtually every European nation between France and Russia, and men from the northern and southern borders of the European continent. This is understandable, given that at the start of the war, military confrontations between the world powers had become so common that combat was raised to the status of a fine art, consuming a large portion of time for adolescent males in training and comprising a sizeable component of the economy. Weaponry was developed to a degree of quality not accessible to most North Americans, and European aristocrats were reared in the mastery of swordsmanship with an emphasis on the saber for military use. Likewise, the cavalry, buoyed by a tradition of expert horsemanship and saddle-based combat, was a fighting force largely beyond reach for colonists, which meant that fighting on horses was an undeveloped practice in the fledgling Continental Army, and the American military did not yet fully comprehend the value of cavalry units. Few sword masters were to find their way to North America in time for the war, and the typical American musket was a fair hunting weapon rather than a military one. Even the foot soldier knew little of European military discipline.

All of this helps explain why, aside from George Washington, many Americans are likely able to name just as many foreign generals on the rebel side as American generals. While names like Lafayette, Pulaski, Kościuszko, and Baron von Steuben are quickly associated with the Revolution, American officers like Nathanael Greene, Anthony Wayne, Horatio Gates, Henry Knox, and Light-Horse Harry Lee are often overlooked.

In fact, Wayne was one of early America's most important commanders, from his distinguished service in the Revolutionary War to leading soldiers against various Native American bands along the frontier after America secured its independence. Wayne played critical roles in several of the Revolution's most noteworthy campaigns, from the fateful Quebec invasion of 1775-1776 to the Yorktown campaign that ended the major fighting in 1781, with crucial actions at places like Valley Forge and Stony Point. He had been promoted to Major General by the time the war ended, and when he died near the end of the 18th century while still on active duty, few American military officers had left behind as influential legacy as the daring, but almost always successful general.

Mad Anthony Wayne: The Life and Legacy of the Famous Revolutionary War General profiles one of the Revolutionary War's most famous soldiers. Along with pictures of important people, places, and events, you will learn about Wayne like never before.

Life Before the Revolution

Anthony Wayne was born on January 1, 1745, at his family's Waynesborough estate in Easttown Township, Chester County, Pennsylvania. Wayne was of Anglo-Irish descent, and he descended from a military line back in England that participated in the Glorious Revolution near the end of the 17th century. Chales Stille wrote of Wayne's English ancestry, "The grandfather of the general during the reign of Charles II had removed his family from Yorkshire and had taken possession of an estate in the County Wicklow in Ireland. He was a protestant, and joined the forces of William of Orange in his contest with King James II. He commanded a troop of dragoons in the service of King William at the battle of the Boyne, and he greatly distinguished himself by his gallantry in that decisive battle."

A picture of Waynesborough

Wayne's grandfather and namesake, Anthony Wayne, along with his wife Hannah and eight of their nine children, left County Wicklow in 1722 for Pennsylvania and settled on 1,600 acres that became the Waynesboro estate. At the time, Wayne's father, Isaac Wayne, stayed in England to complete his education before joining the family in Pennsylvania. Horatio Newton Moore described Isaac as "a man of strong mind and of great industry and enterprise." He represented Chester in the Pennsylvania Provincial Assembly, and as a Captain in the Pennsylvania Militia, he participated in skirmishes against local natives.

When he was in his early 40s, Isaac Wayne married Elizabeth Iddings Wayne. Anthony was their first child and their only son out of four children. Isaac desired that Anthony become a farmer, but as the child got older, Isaac decided that farming did not suit his son. Looking to better develop Anthony's mind, Isaac sent Anthony to his brother, Gilbert, a country schoolteacher, for his education. After some time, Gilbert wrote his brother with obvious dissatisfaction, "I really suspect that parental affection blinds you, and that you have mistaken your son's capacity. What he may be best qualified for, I know not. One thing I am certain of, he will never make a scholar. He may perhaps make a soldier. He has already distracted the brains of two-thirds of the boys under my charge, by rehearsals of battles, sieges, etc. They exhibit more the appearance of Indians and Harlequins than students--This one decorated with a cap of many colors; others habited in coats as variegated, like Joseph's of old--some laid up with broken heads and black eyes. During noon, in place of the usual games of amusements, he has the boys employed in throwing up redoubts, skirmishing, etc. I must be candid with you, brother Isaac--unless Anthony pays more attention to his books, I shall be under the painful necessity of dismissing him from the school."

In response, Isaac threatened to take Anthony home and put him back to work on the farm. Taking the threat seriously, Anthony doubled his efforts at his studies, and he became a serious student under his uncle's tutelage. After 18 months, Uncle Gilbert was able to inform his father that Anthony had learned all he could under his direction.

At age 16, Anthony entered Philadelphia Academy, where he excelled at mathematics. After that, he returned to Chester County and opened his own land surveying office, where he gained a reputation as a good surveyor in short order. In 1765, he was employed by a company formed by Benjamin Franklin to make a survey of two tracts of land the organization had purchased in Nova Scotia. Wayne was also charged with establishing a settlement on the tracts to cultivate them. He was specifically told to observe the following about the land: ""[T]he land proposed to be bought and settled upon was, 1. Good & supplied with navigable waters. 2. To observe where were the heads of navigation in Rivers, that is, the tide. 3. Convenient places for ferries. 4. Passes through the mountains, 5. Iron ore & cole mines. 6. Mill Seats & other waterworks. 7. Places where the roads meet. 8. Beaches or islands with black sand washed up. 9. Mast lands or pure swamps. 10. Lime stone or ther stones. 11. Meadow lands and marsh. 12 Large Springs or any mineral Springs."

Franklin

In May 1766, Wayne married Mary Penrose, the daughter of Bartholomew Penrose, and they would go on to have two children, Margretta in 1770 and Isaac in 1772. From the time of his marriage until 1774, he split his time between farming and surveying, and he became so trusted by his neighbors that he was elected to various county offices and became a leader among the colonists agitating against British taxes on the colonies.

In 1763, when Wayne was not yet 20, the British concluded the Seven Years' War with a decisive victory over the French that left France with almost no colonial possessions in North America. Although the Seven Years' War, known as the French and Indian War in the United States, was a crushing defeat for the French and a resounding success for Great Britain, the war itself put the Kingdom deep in debt. To help alleviate the burden, Parliament soon began to pass a number of additional taxes to repay the nation's war debts.

Many of the new taxes targeted the 13 colonies, and the logic for raising revenue in the colonies was clear. After all, the Seven Years' War had begun in North America, and a great deal of Britain's war expenses had gone toward supporting and defending the colonies. Moreover, the colonies were relatively untaxed by Great Britain compared to England, Scotland, and Wales. Finally, no member of Parliament represented the 13 colonies, so Parliament could increase taxes on the colonies without a great deal of Parliamentary opposition or backlash among British citizens.

This last fact, while convenient for Parliament, created a great deal of ill will in the colonies. Many colonists believed that Parliament had no right to raise taxes when the colonies had no representation in Parliament, and they pointed to the fact that the King of England had long since surrendered any claim to raise taxes without the consent of the people's representatives in Parliament. A Parliament without a single American member, the colonists argued, could no more legally raise taxes on them than the King could on British citizens. Taxation without representation was, in the colonists' view, a violation of their rights as Englishmen.

By the time Wayne had advanced professionally, the colonies were becoming increasingly restive under British rule. The Sugar Act of 1764, the Stamp Act of 1765, and the Townshend Acts of 1767 had placed an increasing number of taxes and restrictions on the colonies, ostensibly designed to pay for the protection of the colonies, but colonial legislatures, including that of Virginia, saw these actions by Parliament as infringing on their traditional rights and prerogatives, particularly their sole right to raise and levy taxes within their boundaries.

Infuriated by the Boston Tea Party, which took place in December 1773, Parliament passed a new set of stringent and punitive laws known collectively as the Coercive Acts. The first of these closed the Port of Boston to both coming and going ships, in effect crippling the city's economy until the city repaid the merchants for their lost tea. The second basically invalidated the Massachusetts Charter and gave Parliament the right to appoint colonial officials previously elected by their peers. Next, the Administration of Justice Act authorized judges to remove any colonist charged with a crime to another colony, or even Great Britain, for trial. The final and most severe blow, however, came when Governor Thomas Hutchinson was removed and replaced with General Thomas Gage, commander of the British forces in America, placing the city under unofficial martial law.

With the Coercive or Intolerable Acts of 1774, Parliament hoped the punitive measures would compel the colonies to stop resisting Parliamentary authority. Like the other attempts, however, this one only had the opposite effect, with many colonists viewing the acts as an arbitrary violation of their rights.

Wayne was elected to the Pennsylvania Legislature in 1774 from Chester County, and in the summer of 1775, he was appointed as one of the members of the Committee of Safety with Franklin, John Dickson and others. Committees like these spread out across all of the colonies, and it was through these circles that patriots across the American colonies communicated with each other and would form a united response to what they considered British transgressions. When Samuel Adams and the Bostonians communicated with a committee in New York to suggest a boycott, New York's Committee of 51, dominated by merchants, suggested a different idea. "Upon these reasons we conclude that a congress of deputies from the colonies in general is of the utmost moment; that it ought to be assembled without delay, and some unanimous resolution formed in this fatal emergency, not only respecting your deplorable circumstances, but for the security of our common rights." In this way, the Coercive Acts unintentionally created the first representative body utilized by almost all the colonies: the First Continental Congress.

The 56 delegates who had been chosen by their colonial legislatures to attend the First Continental Congress met to craft a united response to the Intolerable Acts, debate the merits of a boycott of British trade, declare their rights and demand redress. 12 of the original 13 colonies attended the First Continental Congress; Georgia did not, primarily because it was hoping for assistance from the British Army in combating Native Americans who were attacking its frontier.

Beginning on September 5, 1774, in Philadelphia, Pennsylvania, the First Continental Congress started meeting. Its ultimate aim was, of course, respect for North American constitutional rights to representation in Parliament. Meeting in Carpenter's Hall, where Pennsylvania's Congress met, the delegates aimed to show a united force and authority toward Great Britain, but from the beginning this would be tough to accomplish because the different colonies had different priorities. For example, Pennsylvania and New York sent delegates with instructions to seek a cordial and respectful resolution with the British, while others advocated separation between their colony and Britain. Some of the colonies had men with far different views. For example, Virginia's delegates included statesmen like George Washington and Richard Henry Lee, but it also included the fiery Patrick Henry

Furthermore, the objectives of the Congress weren't entirely set out ahead of time, leaving the body to quickly form a leadership and figure out a core set of tasks to carry out. The first few weeks consisted mostly of discussing and debating the issues, and Joseph Galloway of Pennsylvania came up with the first plan, "A Plan of Union of Great Britain and the Colonies", which suggested a popularly elected Grand Council among all of the colonies that would be their equivalent of Parliament. This would eventually be undone by the delegates arriving from Boston, whose ongoing troubles with the British made them much more pessimistic about an effort at conciliation.

On October 14, 1774, the Declaration and Resolves established the Congress' statement of principles, which they considered as common principles for all of the colonies. It was also on this day that Congress voted to meet again the following year if these grievances were not attended to by England. Once that body convened, however, its purpose proved to be very different.

About a week later, the Congress formed The Association on October 20, which was the pact for boycotting English goods. The Association also meant to establish processes throughout the colonies that could regulate resistance and keep it united, as well as improving communication among the colonies.

All of the state legislatures except Georgia and New York had their legislative bodies approve of the measures created in Congress. The demands were then sent to Parliament, but Congress received no response. By mid-1775, imports from Britain dropped an astounding 97%, indicating a highly effective boycott of British goods. Events in the interim months, of course, had greatly affected the reduced trade between Britain and its colonies, given that war had broken out in the wake of the fighting at Lexington and Concord that April.

The Start of the Revolutionary War

"I shall begin my march for Camp tomorrow morning. It was not in my power to move until I could procure shoes for the troops almost barefoot." – Anthony Wayne

For his part, Wayne preferred military service, and he began making what he considered the necessary preparations to take up the sword and lead his fellow colonists in battle. He read widely in military history and tactics, and in September 1775, he resigned from the Pennsylvania Assembly and the Committee of Safety to raise a regiment of volunteers for service. He was commissioned the Colonel of the 4th Pennsylvania Regiment on January 3, 1776. Stille explained, "During the winter of 1776 Wayne was engaged at Chester in preparing his men for active service, and in bringing them under proper discipline. He began by punishing desertion severely. Before his regiment left Pennsylvania no less than six of its members were punished, some with fifteen and others with thirty-nine lashes for this offence."

Wayne's first military campaign of the Revolution was one of its most notorious. After Benedict Arnold and Ethan Allen captured Fort Ticonderoga in 1775, General Washington assigned Arnold command of an expedition to the British stronghold Quebec via the Maine wilderness. Arnold's command would meet up with another expedition starting out from Ticonderoga, and together the two forces were to attack Quebec.

Arnold

The first expedition to set out was led by Philip Schuyler, who fell ill and turned command over to brigadier-general Richard Montgomery. That group, which included several thousand locally raised militia, laid siege to Fort St. Johns on September 17, capturing supplies and cutting off its line of communications with Montreal. However, they were set back by the capture of Ethan Allen a week later, when Allen rashly tried to attack Montreal instead of merely raising more soldiers as ordered.

Schuyler

Montgomery's troops eventually captured Montreal and began setting forth for Quebec City. Meanwhile, Arnold started out from around present-day Augusta, Maine, and it was an ill-fated journey from the beginning. As he tried to move his nearly 1,100 strong force up the Kennebec River, the forces were plagued with leaky boats that ruined gunpowder and food supplies. Marching over land was no easier since the area was a mixture of swampy marshes, lakes and rivers. And by making the march in winter, the poor weather convinced nearly a quarter of Arnold's men to turn around.

By the time Arnold reached the St. Lawrence River in November, he had 600 men struggling with disease and starvation, but Arnold had somehow managed to get them 400 miles to the objective. Not surprisingly, Quebec refused to surrender to Arnold's ragtag force, even after they demanded a surrender, and Arnold wisely waited to link up with Montgomery's men.

After being joined then by Montgomery's forces from Montreal, Canada, they together lodged repeated attacks, all of which failed to penetrate British defenses. During what would become known as the Battle of Quebec, staged on December 31, 1775 in near-blizzard conditions, General Montgomery was killed and Colonel Arnold severely wounded in the leg. Though Arnold kept up a siege until March 1776 while Congress debated whether to continue offensive operations in the area, Quebec could never be taken.

To aid Arnold's invasion, Wayne's 4th Regiment was part of a Pennsylvania Brigade led by General William Thompson. Wayne's 4th, along with the 2nd Regiment under Colonel Arthur St. Clair and the 6th Regiment under Colonel William Irvine, were among the forces sent by the Continental Congress to reinforce Arnold in the wake of the Battle of Quebec. Such was the situation that some companies of Wayne's regiment were hurried towards the front without arms, and it was not until they reached Albany, New York in the first week of May 1776 that those were provided. Five companies under Lieutenant-Colonel Francis Johnston were kept on Long Island until May 15, and even then armed only with tomahawks.

The force finally reached the fort at the mouth of the Sorel in Canada, halfway between Montreal and Quebec, on June 5, and found the remnant of the forces under the overall command of General John Sullivan. Sullivan ordered Thompson to take the Pennsylvania Brigade and attack the British forces under General Burgoyne then gathered at Three Rivers.

This was Wayne's first battle, and he later recounted it in a letter to Benjamin Franklin: "DEAR SIR,-After a long march by land & water varied with Delightful as well as Gloomy prospects we arrived here the night of the 5th Instant and on the 7th it was agreed in a council of war to attack the enemy at Three Rivers about 47 miles lower down, whose strength was estimated at 3 or 4 Hundred. Gen'l Thompson was appointed for this Command, the Disposition was as follows 4 attacks to be made at the same time viz Col Maxwell to conduct the first, myself the second, Col St Clair the third, & Col Irvine the 4th Lie't Col Hartley the Reserves. On the same evening we Embarked and arrived at Col St Clairs Encampment about midnight—it was intended that the Attack shou'd be made at the dawn of day—this we found to be Impracticable, therefor we Remained where we were until the 9th when we to the number of 1450 Men all Penns'lvanians except Maxwells Battalion took boats About 2 in the morning we landed nine Miles above the town, and after an Hour's march day began to appear. Our Guides had mistook the road, the Enemy Discovered and Cannonaded us from their ships, a Surprise was out of the Question—we therefore put our best face on it and Continued our line of march thro' a thick deep swamp three miles wide, and after four Hours Arrived at a more open piece of Ground—amidst the thickest firing of the ship ping when all of a sudden a large Body of Regulars marched down in good Order Immediately in front of me to prevent our forming-- in Consequence of which I Ordered my Light Infantry together with Capt Hay's Company of Riflemen to advance and amuse them whilst I was forming; they began and Continued the attack with great spirit until I advanced to support them when I ordered them to wheel to the Right & left and flank the Enemy at the same time we poured in a well Aimed and heavy fire in front as this— they attempted to Retreat in good Order enemy. at first but in a few minutes broke and ran N / in the utmost Confusion. About this time - the Other Divisions began to Emerge from the swamp except Maxwell who with his was advanced in a thicket a Considerable Distance to the left—our Rear now becoming our front &c. At this Instant we Rec'd a heavy fire in flank from musketry, field pieces, Howitzers &c. &c. which threw us into some confusion, but was Instantly Remedied— We Advanced in Column up to their breast work's which till then we had not

Discovered—at this time Gen'l Thompson with Cols St Clair, Irvine & Hartly were marching in full view to our support. Col Maxwell now began to Engage on the left of me, the fire was so hot he could not maintain his post—the other troops had also filed off to the left—my small Battalion composed of my own & two Companies of Jersey men under Major Ray amounting in the whole to about 200 were left exposed to the whole fire of the shipping in flank and full three thousand men in front with all their Artillery under the command of Gen'l Burgoyne— Our people taking example by others gave way— Indeed it was Impossible for them to stand it longer— Whilst Col Allen and myself were Employed in Rallying the troops Let. Col. Hartly had advanced with the Reserves and bravely Attacked the Enemy from a thicket in a swamp to the left, this hardiness of his was of the Utmost Consequence to us—we having rallied about 8oo men from the Different Regiments —we now sent to find the Gen'l and Other field Officers—at the same time the Rifle men of mine & Irvine's kept up a galling fire on the Enemy—the Swamp was so deep and thick with timber and underwood that a man Io yards in front or Rear wou'd not see the men Drawn up—this was the Cause of the Gen'l, Col St Clair, Maxwell & Irvine missing us—or perhaps they had taken for Granted that we were all cut off—Col Hartly who lay nearby retreated without a Discovery on either side, until he Crossed our line near the left, which caused our people to follow him—Allen and myself were now left on the field with only twenty men & five Officers, the Enemy still Continuing their whole fire from Great and small guns upon us— but afraid to venture from their lines, we thought it prudent to keep them in play by keeping up a small fire in Order to gain time for our people to make good their Retreat in Consequence of which we Continued about an Hour longer in the field, and then Retreated back into the woods which brought us to a Road on the far side of the Swamp. We followed this Road about two miles when we cut loose from our small party & reached the Place where our people had enter'd the swamp by which means we soon Collected 6 or 7oo men with whom we Retreated in good Order but without nourishment of any kind. The Enemy who were Strong in number had Detached in two or three bodies about 15oo men to cut off our Retreat. They waylaid & Engaged us again about 9 miles from the field of Battle, they did us little damage. We Continued our march, and the third day almost worn out with fatigue, Hunger, & Difficulties, scarcely to be paralleled we arrived here with 11oo men, but Gen'l Thompson Col Irvine Doc'r McCalla and several Officers are prisoners at Three Rivers— Col St Clair Arrived alone last night Their Separation from the Army (which appeared Indeed to be lost) was the cause of their misfortunes—I believe it will be Universally allowed that Col Allen & myself have saved the Army in Canada. Capt Robinson has proved himself the Soldier and the Gen'tm. his Conduct has outgone the most Sanguine hopes of his friends, out of 150 of my own I have lost more than the One Quarter part—together with Slight touch in my Right leg—which is partly well already, we shall have more business soon, our People are in high spirits and long for the Other bought as well as your H'l S't— ANT'Y WAYNE."

After the battle, the beaten rebel forces retreated from Quebec back south, and one of Wayne's roles was to cover the escape of Arnold from Montreal. General Sullivan's aide-de-camp, James Wilkinson, recounted Wayne's participation in the retreat: "I found every house and hut on my route crowded with straggling men without officers, and officers without men. The first officer of my acquaintance whom I met was Lieutenant Colonel William Allen, of the Second Pennsylvania. I informed him of my orders for a detachment. He replied, 'Wilkinson, this army is conquered by its fears, and I doubt whether you can draw any assistance from it; but Colonel Wayne is in the rear, and if any one can do it he is the man.' On which I quickened my pace, and half an hour after I met that gallant soldier as much at his ease as if he was marching to a parade of exercise. He halted at the bridge and posted a guard, with orders to stop every man, without regard to corps, who appeared to be active, alert, and equipped. In a short time a detachment was completely formed and in motion for Longueil (on the route to Montreal). The very men who only the day before were retreating in confusion before a division of the enemy now marched with alacrity against his main body." Shortly afterwards it was discovered that Arnold had escaped without the aid of Wayne's troops, and they were pushed on to join Sullivan. "Then," says Wilkinson, "our detachment was discovered advancing on the bank of the Sorel two miles below the fort. We were taken (by Sullivan) for the enemy, and great alarm and confusion ensued, the drums beat to arms, and General Sullivan and his officers were observed making great exertions to prepare for battle. Colonel Wayne halted his column, pulled out his glass, and seemed to enjoy the panic his appearance produced."

Sullivan

Though the invasion was an abject failure, Wayne had distinguished himself during the operations in Canada. His performance was brought to the attention of General Philip Schuyler, who appointed Wayne to command Fort Ticonderoga, a garrison of over 2,000 men, on November 18, 1776.

During his time there, he regularly corresponded with his wife and friends in Pennsylvania about the conditions there. He wrote his wife in January 1777, "DEAR Polly,–I don't know where this will meet you. The Rapid progress of the Enemy through Jersey only reach'd us last evening—perhaps they may now be in Phil'a and Ravaging the Country for many miles Round The Anxiety we are under on acc't of our families and friends is much better felt than expressed— Should you be necessitated to leave Easttown—I doubt not but you'l meet with Hospitality in the Back parts of the provinces— The British Rebels may be successful for a time; they may take and Destroy our Towns near the Water and Distress us much But they never can— they never will subjugate the free born sons of America. Our Growing Country can meet with Considerable Losses and survive them : but one Defeat to our more than Savage Enemy Ruins them for ever: A number of unhappy Circumstances have Contributed to their success thus far, but let not that in the least Dispirit you. We shall soon learn to face them in the field and the day is not far off when we shall produce a Conviction to the World that we Deserve to be free— I expect every hour to be Relieved with Orders to march to the Assistance of Gen'l Washington: I have 15oo Hardy Veterans left who will push hard for Victory and Revenge—they are second to none in Courage (I have seen them tried) and I know they Equal any Regulars in point of Discipline—I hope soon to meet their Sanguine Wish—that is to lead them on to Death or Glory Kiss my little boy and Girl for me— Give my kindest Compliments to all friends."

Shortly after writing that letter to his wife, Wayne wrote General Schuyler, "DEAR GENERAL,-I herewith send you a Return of this Garrison as also of the Soldiers re-engaged to serve during the War—which are but few— "Liberty to come down for one month when Relieved" carries with it an Idea of being Immediately sent back again to a place which they Imagine to be very unhealthy;—they say; march us off this Ground and then we will Cheerfully Re-engage; add to this their anxiety about their friends in the Jerseys and Penns'a makes them Impatient to be led to the assistance of their Distressed Country They likewise see the Eastern people Running away in the Clouds of the Night—(some before and all soon as their times expires). Col Whitcombs Regiment—all the Sailors & Mariners—the whole of the Artificers and all the Corps of Artillery except Capt. Roman's Company (which consists but of 12 men Officers Included) are gone off the Ground Notwithstanding so bad an example—and the distress of their native State—the Pennsylvanians, will not leave me until fresh troops arrive to Relieve themYour own feelings Sir on the Alarming Situation of Affairs in Penns'a and Jersey; will best Inform you of that of every Other Officer and Soldier (from those States) on the Present Occasion : which causes us most Ardently to wish for an Opportunity of meeting those Sons of War and Rapine—face to face; and man to man. These worthy fellows are Second to none in Courage (I have seen them proved)—and I know that they are not far behind any Regulars in

Point of Discipline— Such troops, actuated by Principle, and fired with just Resentment must be an Acceptable, and perhaps season able Reinforcement to Gen'l Washington at this Critical Juncture— If you shou'd be of the same Opinion and cause us to be Immediately relieved—with Orders to march with all Dispatch to join the main Army—I believe we shou'd be able to Re-enlist the Chief part of our people on the way: however this may be I wou'd answer for it that they will not turn aside from Danger (altho their terms shou'd be expired) when the safety and Honor of their Country Require them to face it— I must Once more earnestly Request you to Order up shoes and soap—we are much Distressed for want of these Necessary Articles— Doct'r M'Crea arrived last night with some Medicine—but Hospital Stores, roots and Vegetables we are totally Destitute of."

Later that same month, Wayne appraised Schuyler of the situation of the fort, which he wrote of in stark terms while complimenting the troops under his command: "DEAR GEN'L,-Col Simons Reg't Col Robinsons Reg't Consisting of about 700 men Officers Included are now Arrived together with 24 men of Col Warner's Regiment— In Consequence I have Ordered One Reg't of the Penns'a to march tomorrow. The Others will follow as soon as Possible with Orders to Proceed in Good Order to Phil'a— I have Lately Rec'd letters from Gen'l St. Clair and other Gent'm in Gen'l Washing ton's Camp which made me think it Advisable to keep these Regt's Embodied until they are Dismissed by the Board of War:—their time expired the 5th of this Instant: they are to be settled within Phil'a agreeable to Promise, when I have Reason to expect the greatest part will Reengage— I want much to go also—it would be in my Power to do more with them in case of necessity than perhaps any other Officer: I know these worthy fellows well and they know me— I am Confident they would not Desert me in a time of Danger— If you think it would be for the benefit of the Service—I shou'd be glad to be Immediately Relieved in Command with Orders to march with the last of the Southern troops. For the present I am using every Effort to Render this place strong. I shall soon Complete the Abattis Round the Old fort, and Octagons on Mt. Independence, and two New Blockhouses; so that in a few days we hope to Render this post tenable and leave it in a much securer and better state than we found it—the manner in which I have kept our Guards and Sentries and the Constant Succession of Scouts which I have out—if followed by my successor—will Effect ually prevent a surprise; you will please to Order the Other troops Destin'd for this Garrison to be forward'd with all Possible Dispatch"

In February 1777, he wrote to his friend Sharp Delany, "I must now in Confidence tell you that this post has been most shamefully neglected—all the old and good Troops are gone—none here but a few wretched militia—badly armed and worse Disciplined— This Garrison at this time Ought to Consist of at least 50oo Effective men—with a well trained Corps of Artillery— perhaps Congress thinks it does. I have not One fifth part of that number on the Ground—and I would much Rather Risque my life, Reputation, and the fate of America on 4oo Good Troops, than the Whole of the present Garrison. This is the Situation of the Second post in the United States— the Neighboring Governments are now roused—and I expect in a few days to be strongly Re-enforced— A body of the Enemy were Discovered a few days since marching this way by two Canadians— who are gone to Albany—this has awaked Gen'l Schuyler and Others (whose business it was to send Troops) from their Lethargy— We may probably have some Diversion in a few Hours—I have yet some good men on whom I can Depend—and I will be answerable for the maintenance of this post until succour can Arrive."

Delany

While he remained at Ticonderoga, Wayne was promoted to the rank of Brigadier-General on February 21, 1777. In March, his friend Sharp Delaney wrote to congratulate him and expressed hope that he would soon return to Pennsylvania: "My DEAR GENERAL,-To wish my Friend Joy or congratulate him on his advancement to the Rank of B: General, would seem as if I did not thoroughly know him—but to me your merits are sufficiently known I am firmly persuaded that office could not be better or more properly given—&' ought long ere now– Your last gave me true friendly pain—since Sept'r & not a line from Family or Friends when to my knowledge you ought to have rec'd many— Yesterday I came from East-town & left all very well tho strong in expectation of your long wished arrival— Tho' I share in every one of your honours—yet believe me I could wish you had not left us—more may be done by you in the distracted state of our Government—than perhaps would balance the many gallant & beneficial actions you have done for your Country in Canada. To point them out in a letter would be impossible which is the reason I have but slightly touched on them in former letters. When I have the great pleasure to see you here—I shall give you a long talk, showing the weakness, folly, Ambition of politicians. Before matters are brought right you may be Witness, you must be witness to all of them. I never yet flattered myself you could have been spared on Acct of the Importance of the Post you command—till properly relieved, —tho all other of your friends were sure of your coming— Gen'l Greene a few days since informed me a G'l Patterson was to take charge of Ticond'a chiefly for your coming home which only gives me the hope of seeing you—busy scenes may perhaps induce you to give your Services to your Country without any intermission—but let me my Friend, advise & beg of you, to come first home, & gratify your Friends & put new life in your Family & Mother who really pine for the beloved Husband, Father & Son. You are the only military man I know who has been so long on Duty—nor is it to be expected or thought the whole man should or could be absorbed by one line of Duty—come then once more let me ask it, & speedily to your desiring Friends, & in a time we will again restore you to the Continent. I have need of you myself for many accounts— I have been in the field, if to be as I was may be called so—would to God our militia were better regulated— I was honoured by the Assembly with the Post of Lieu't of the City with Rank of Col'l Command't so that you see I may have been at head of the militia of our State but declined it—for reasons I know will be pleasing to you, when I can see and converse with you.”

The Times that Try Men's Souls

“Our officers and men behaved like men who are determined to be free.” – Anthony Wayne

Although Wayne wrote pessimistically about the conditions at Ticonderoga in letters to acquaintances, he was still confident that the position could not be taken by the British without a bloody fight, and he expressed that to his superiors. In part because of that confidence, Wayne would be ordered to leave the fort in early 1777 to help Washington elsewhere.

After the Continental Army's successful siege of Boston finished in early 1776, Washington suspected that the British evacuated by sea to New York City, the next logical target in an attempt to end a colonial resurrection. He thus rushed his army south to defend the city, and though he guessed correctly, it would be to no avail. Unlike Boston, New York City's terrain featured few defensible positions. Moreover, Washington wasn't sure defending the city was necessary, hoping that an expedition launched toward Quebec like the one Benedict Arnold had led would keep the British away from New York. But Congress thought otherwise and demanded that Washington defend New York.

Washington thus did what he was told, and it nearly resulted in his army's demise. In the summer of 1776, the British conducted the largest amphibious expedition in North America's history at the time, landing over 20,000 troops on Long Island. British General William Howe, who had led the British at Bunker Hill and would later become commander in chief of the armies in North America, easily captured Staten Island, which Washington was incapable of defending without a proper navy. Washington's army attempted to fight, but Washington was badly outmaneuvered, and his army was nearly cut off from escape, and his withdrawal across New York City was enormously disorderly, with many of Washington's troops so scared that they deserted. Others were sick, with dysentery and smallpox plaguing the Continental Army in New York. In what was arguably the worst defeat of the Revolution, Washington was ashamed. He also felt betrayed, by both his troops and Congress.

To escape from New York, Washington led a tactical retreat across the East River and off Long Island in the middle of the night without British knowledge. This retreat prevented the annihilation of the colonial army in New York, but with Washington being pushed west across New Jersey and into Pennsylvania, Congress was forced to flee Philadelphia. And with this string of crucial British successes in 1776, the Revolution was on the brink of failure.

The Continental Army, now in Pennsylvania, had lost over 5,000 men during its retreat through New York and New Jersey and now had fewer than 5,000 able soldiers. That winter, one of the men in camp, Thomas Paine, would write *The American Crisis*, beginning with the famous words, "These are the times that try men's souls."

After New York, Washington's forces were in bad shape. The colonial forces would never prove a match for the heavily experienced redcoats in a pitched battle, but now their morale was at an all time low, and Washington also had to worry about much of his army leaving after their enlistments expired at the end of the year.

After failing to bag Washington's army in New York, the British gave chase, but with the winter beginning, the British camped out on the New Jersey side of the Delaware River. In the 18th century, armies generally suspended their ongoing military campaigns during winter, allowing the colonists to plan ways to halt British momentum during the fighting months. A perfect example of that was Benedict Arnold's campaign to Quebec in 1775, which was a tactical defeat that succeeded in keeping the British in Canada from conducting a campaign until the spring of 1776.

With a beaten down army, American morale was low. Throughout all the colonies, many expressed doubts about the viability of the war. Washington knew he needed a big victory, after having spent the past six months suffering one defeat after the other. On the other hand, it seemed perfectly logical to camp out in Pennsylvania and wait until spring to resume fighting. But Washington's insistence on a big move was so resolute that he authorized an unorthodox decision on Christmas of 1776.

On Christmas night, Washington led his troops across the frigid and partially frozen Delaware

River. Once on the other side, they advanced south to Trenton, where they attacked, captured and killed Hessian soldiers stationed there. The Hessians had celebrated Christmas and were completely unprepared for an attack. Only a handful of Americans were killed, while the Continental Army captured over 1,000 Hessian forces, and killed nearly 100.

Leutz's famous painting of Washington crossing the Delaware

The Battle of Trenton was indeed the decisive move Washington had hoped it would be. The British general, Lord Cornwallis, marched south from New York City through New Jersey to capture Trenton. Washington, however, moved to Cornwallis's rear and attacked the British at Princeton, New Jersey in January 1777, forcing the British to retreat to New York City for the rest of the winter.

Despite the victory, however, Washington faced an unprecedented crisis. Apart from the men recruited in Massachusetts before the creation of the Second Continental Congress, Washington's Army's 1-year recruitment term was now up. With the end of the year 1776, much of Washington's Army intended to finish. Washington had to urge Congress to make an important decision and extend enlistment terms. Fearing the creation of a permanent Army, many in Congress feared making this decision. In the end, however, they approved enlistment terms of three years or "until the war is finished." Crisis had been narrowly averted, at least for now.

Thus, at the end of 1776, the American war effort was on the verge of collapse, and despite Washington's success at Trenton, the British were confident that they could quell the rebellion in 1777. That winter, the British planned a complicated campaign in which British armies from Canada and New York would strike out across New England and link up, with the goal of cutting off the Northern colonies. Indeed, 1777 did prove to be the pivotal year of the war, but not in the way the British intended.

The British planned a three-pronged sweep through the northern colonies that would eventually end with the linking of three different forces. The design of the plan called for the capture of Philadelphia, as well as the colony of New York, and it aimed all but slice the rebellious colonies in two.

Burgoyne

This was the situation when Wayne received orders from Washington on April 12, 1777 to join him at Morristown, New Jersey. There, Washington placed him in command of the brigade of troops from Pennsylvania, known as the Pennsylvania Line. Stille provided the order of battle for the Pennsylvania Line: "The command to which General Wayne was as signed in the spring of 1777 was, as has been said, composed of eight regiments, forming a division of two brigades. The First Brigade consisted of the First Regiment, Colonel Chambers; the Second, Colonel Walter Stewart; the Seventh, Lieutenant-Colonel Con nor; and the Tenth, Lieutenant-Colonel Hubley. The Second Brigade was composed of the Fourth Regiment, Lieutenant-Colonel William Butler; the Fifth, Lieutenant-Colonel Johnston; the Eighth, Colonel Broadhead; and the Eleventh, Colonel Humpton. There were about seventeen hundred men in the division when

General Wayne assumed the command. The other division of the Pennsylvania line in Washington's army, under Lord Stirling's command, was made up of Conway's— formerly Mifflin's—brigade of four regiments, and of Colonel Hausegger's German regiment."

The first action Wayne took with his new command was an assault on a British detachment at Brunswick on May 2. Wayne described the action in a letter to the Board of War: "GENTLEMEN,+In Consequence of the Orders of His Excellency Gen'l Washington I now send Major Miller for Arms & Clothing for the first Penn'a Regiment Commanded by Col. Chambers—they never Rec'd any Uniform except hunting Shirts which are worn out —and Altho a body of fine men—yet from being in Rags and badly armed—they are viewed with Contempt by the Other Troops, and begin to Despise themselves—Discontent ever produces Desertion, to prevent which I must in the most pressing manner Request you to Assist him and the Other Gentlemen who go on the same Errand in procuring Clothes and Arms. The Conduct of the Pennsylvanians the Other day in forceing Gen'l Grant to Retire with Circumstances of Shame and Disgrace into the very lines of the Enemy has gained them the Esteem and Confidence of His Excellency—who wishes to have Our Rifles ex changed for good Muskets & Bayonets—experience has taught us that they are not fit for the field—a few only will be Retained in each Regiment and those placed in the hands of Real Marksmen.— I have taken this Liberty as I am Confident that you have the Honor of your State at Heart—and that you will use every means in your Power to expedite the Arming & Clothing of our People as Soldiers in Order to support it—"

As confident as he was in the rightness of the patriot cause and the ultimate success of Washington's efforts, he did express a more serious tone to his wife in a letter he wrote her in June 1777: "My DEAR Polly,–I this moment Rec'd yours of the 31st May— and am extremely sorry to hear of your bad state of health—you must Endeavor to keep up your Spirits as well as possible—the times Require great Sacrifices to be made—the Blessings of Liberty can not be purchased at too high a price—the Blood and treasure of the Choicest and best Spirits of this Land is but a trifling Consideration for the Rich Inheritance— Whether any of the present leaders will live to see it Established in this Once happy Soil Depends on Heaven;—but it must, it will at one day rise in America, & shine forth in its pristine Lustre. I would advise you to use every possible Endeavour to get in your Harvest yourself and not put it Out on Shares on no Acc't as grain and Hay will be at a Prodigious price next winter. Have we no kind Neighbours to lend a helping hand P-I am sure the Bartholomews & Davis's families will have goodness Enough to give you their Assistance and Advice,—present my best Respects to them and all our friends & tell them they live in my grateful Memory—and that I hope at one day to Enjoy peace, Established on the firm Basis of Liberty in their Social Company The Education of my Little Children is a matter that gives me much Concern—and which I [hope] you will not neglect—I have already hinted [that] I expect my little son will not turn aside from virtue, though the path should be marked with his father's Blood–"

By July, Burgoyne had taken Fort Ticonderoga in New York, but as he tried to get a bearing on the coordinated strategy, the Americans shot another hole into the grand campaign at Fort Stanwix. The British and their Native American allies had inflicted some serious damage on militiamen near Fort Stanwix, but Arnold led an 800-man contingent to the outskirts of the fort and began to lay siege. Realizing that he would not win an open battle, Arnold resorted to subterfuge and succeeded into fooling the British allied Native Americans that he had a much larger force. When the British were left without their allies, Colonel Anthony St. Leger decided to head back toward Quebec. His men would never link up with Burgoyne's as planned.

Receiving word that General William Howe had departed from New York, and concerned he was intent on landing near Philadelphia, Washington issued the following order to Wayne on July 25: "The fleet having gone out of the Hook, and as Delaware appears to be its most probable destination, I desire that you will leave your brigade under the next in command, and proceed to Chester County, in Pennsylvania, where your presence will be necessary to arrange the militia who are to rendezvous there."

While on his way, Wayne wrote to his wife on August 26, "MY DEAR GIRL,~I am peremptorily forbid by His Excellency to leave the Army—my case is hard— I am Obliged to do the duty of three General Officers—but if it was not the case—as a Gen'l Officer I could not Obtain leave of Absence— I must therefore in the most pressing Manner Request you to meet me tomorrow Evening at Naamans Creek—pray bring Mr. Robinson with my Little Son & Daughter along— It may probably happen that we may stay in that Neighbourhood for a day or two."

At the end of August, Burgoyne learned that St. Leger would not be linking up with him, and that he could not expect help from Howe near New York City or Philadelphia. Nevertheless, while worried about where he would camp his army for the winter, Burgoyne decided to keep advancing in September. Thus, instead of heading back to Ticonderoga, Burgoyne made Albany his target for winter camping, and he ordered his army forward until they were just a few miles north of Saratoga by mid-September.

Meanwhile, with his forces encamped near Wilmington, Delaware, Wayne made a reconnaissance of the British lines and their approach towards Pennsylvania. Based in part on this, Washington decided after some consideration to meet the British in open battle on the eastern side of the Brandywine River.

On September 2, Wayne wrote Washington an outline of a proposed expedition against the British, with himself in command of the attack. His tactics and historical references reflected his wide reading of military matters and history he had undertaken before taking command of the 4th Regiment: "SIR,--I took the liberty some days since to suggest the selecting 2500 or 3000 of our best Armed and most Disciplined Troops (exclusive of the Reserves) who should hold themselves in Readiness on the Approach of the Enemy to make a Regular and Vigorous Assault on their Right or Left flank—or such part of their Army as should then be thought most expedient—and not wait the Attack from them— This, Sir, I am well Convinced would Surprise them much—from a persuasion that you dare not leave your Works—it would totally stop the Other part from Advancing—and should the Attack be fortunate—which I have not the least doubt of the Enemy would have no Other Alternative than to Retreat—for they dare not hazard any new manoeuvre in the face of your Army which would be cool & ready to take every Advantage of either their Confusion, Disorder or Retreat—& from which the best and greatest Consequences might be Derived— This Sir is no new Idea—it has been often practiced with success (among many Others) by Casar at Amiens when besieged by the Gauls, who Carried part of the entrenchments and were rendering themselves Masters of the parapet—when he sallied out with his Cohorts—threw them into the utmost Consternation & Obtained an easy Victory— He practiced the same manoeuvre at Alesia against the same people. —Success Justified the Measure—they were struck with a terror & surprise, which Marshal Saxe Justly Observes "proceeds from that Consternation which is the Unavoidable effect of Sudden and unexpected Events" This is a General rule in war; that the Irresistible Impulse of the Human Heart, which is governed by mere momentary Caprice and Opinion—Determines the fate of the day in all Actions;–& as similar Causes Generally produce Similar Effects—I could wish to see it practiced (not only on this Occasion) but to carry it still further —and make the Assault on the Enemy without Risquing too much The Spirit and Numbers of your Regular Troops aided by the Crowds of Militia now Drawing to your Camp, Renders success probable & will at all events be sufficient to guard against any bad Consequences in case of a Military Check by throwing themselves into the works and Strong Ground in your Rear— I own Sir that I dread the Re-embarquing of the Enemy much more than any Consequence attending an Attack upon them for should they take shiping again and proceed to some Other Quarter without Attempting anything this way—you will suffer more in the march after them than you would probably do in a severe Action— besides the Certain loss of the present Militia— Should I be happy enough to meet your Excellency in Opinion— I wish to be of the number Assigned for this business."

Washington did not adopt Wayne's proposal, nor did he put Wayne in command of the attack. Instead, Wayne's Pennsylvania Line was deployed on the left of the American line on the east bank of the Brandywine along with the 3rd Virginia Regiment and the Continental Artillery Regiment (composed of Pennsylvanians) commanded by Colonel Thomas Proctor. The forces were posted at Chad's Ford, where the Brandywine was fordable. Opposite Wayne were the Hessian forces of General Wilhelm von Knyphausen, about 6,000 men overall.

Stille summarized Wayne's actions in the battle: "Wayne had in front of him, separated by a narrow creek, the forces of Knyphausen (the Hessian general), consisting of about seven thousand men, and during the whole day stood his ground firmly, repelling successfully every attempt by Knyphausen to pass the creek, and sending Maxwell with his light infantry occasionally to the other side with orders to annoy him. Wayne remained in this position until sunset, and until the division of Sullivan (reinforced by that of Greene), which had not been able to withstand the attack of Cornwallis, was forced back from Birmingham Meeting House. The right flank of the army being turned by the enemy exposed Wayne's division to the danger of being attacked by Knyphausen in his front and by Cornwallis in his rear. He therefore retreated, as his supports had been driven from the field, to avoid being surrounded. His men were in good order and discipline, and quite ready to attack the tired battalions of the British army had they undertaken to interrupt the retreat of the army. There can be no doubt that his division on this retreat saved the remnant of Sullivan's force."

Of Wayne's actions, General Armstrong latter wrote in his account of the battle, "The firing on the left being the signal for Knyphausen to act, that officer began his movements accordingly; but, notwithstanding the weight and vigor of his attack and the aid it received from a covering battery, he was unable to drive Wayne from his position till near sunset."

Despite the rebels' efforts, the battle resulted in the defeat of the Continental Army, and with that, the path to Philadelphia lay open for the British. After retreating from Brandywine, Washington rallied and regrouped to make another attempt to stall the British advance on Philadelphia. Wayne was ordered to take up a position between the Paoli and the Warren Taverns on the Lancaster Road, and his forces were to harass the British and if possible capture their baggage train. Unfortunately, Loyalist spies in the area betrayed Wayne's position to the British, and on the night of September 20, an overwhelming British force attacked Wayne's camp. The Battle of Paoli was essentially a massacre, and accusations that he had permitted his camp to be surprised left Wayne's reputation severely damaged.

In the wake of the attack, Wayne wrote Washington on September 21, "DEAR GENERAL,- About 11 o'Clock last Evening we were alarmed by a firing from one of our Out guards—The Division was Immediately formed which was no sooner done than a firing began on our Right Flank— I thought proper to order the Division to file off by the Left except the Infantry and two or three Regiments nearest to where the attack began in order to favour our Retreat— By this Time the Enemy and we were not more than Ten Yards Distant—a well directed fire mutually took Place, followed by a charge of Bayonet— numbers fell on each side— We then drew off a Little Distance and formed a Front to oppose to theirs— They did not think Prudent to push matters further. Part of the Division were a little scattered but are Collecting fast— We have saved all our Artillery, Ammunition & Stores except one or two waggons belonging to the Commissary's Department— Gen'l Smallwood was on his march but not within supporting distance he Order'd his people to file off toward this place where his Division and my own now lay— As soon as we have refreshed our Troops for an Hour or Two, we shall follow the Enemy who I this moment learn from Major North, are marching for Schuylkil— I cant as yet ascertain our Loss—but will make out a Return as soon as Possible, our Dead will be collected & buried this Afternoon— I must in Justice to Col's Hart ley, Humpton, Broadhead, Grier, Butler, Hubley & indeed every Field & Other Officer inform your Excellency that I derived every assistance possible from those Gent'n on this Occasion— Whilst I am writing I received yours of the 20th pr. Messrs Dunlap & Leam ing with the Intelligence you wished to Communicate–"

A depiction of the fighting at Paoli

   Washington convened a court of inquiry at Wayne's request to review his conduct at Paoli. Not satisfied with the findings, which called into question some of his decisions, Wayne wrote Washington, "After this state of facts which I pledge my Honor as a Soldier and a Gentleman to give full and Ample proof of I appeal to Your Excellencys own feelings whether I can be easy under so severe and unjust a Charge— I must therefore beg an Immediate trial by a Gen'l Court Martial Your Compliance will much Oblige your Excellencys Most Ob't and Very Humb Ser't."

   Washington assented, and Wayne made a very detailed defense of his actions, summing things up with the following: "Let me put a Question—Suppose after all these Repeated Orders from His Excellency—and the Arrival of Gen'l Smallwood I had Retreated, before I knew whether the Enemy Intended to Attack me or not, and that they should have Marched for the Schuylkill that Morning [which they Actually did]—would not these very Gentlemen have been the first to default me—would not His Excellency with the Greatest Justice have Ordered me in Arrest for Cowardice and Disobedience of his Repeated peremptory and pointed Orders— would I not have stood Culpable in the eyes of the World—would I not Justly merit either Immediate Death or Cashiering? I Certainly would—what line could I follow but that which I did, what more could be done on the Occation than what was done—the Artillery Amunition &c. &c. were Covered and Saved by a body of Brave troops which were Rallied and Remained on the Ground with me for more than an hour after that Gent'n had Effected his Escape from Danger tho' perhaps not without Confusion—I hold it needless to say more on the Occation—I rest my Honor, Character which to me is more Dear than life in the Hands of Gentlemen—who when Deciding on my Honor will not forget their own—"

The court-martial unanimously found that General Wayne was "not guilty of the charge exhibited against him, but that he, on the night of the 20th of September last, did every duty that could be expected from an active, brave and vigilant officer, under the orders which he then had. The Court do acquit him with the highest honor." Washington accepted the decision, and Wayne's conduct was vindicated.

After Paoli, Wayne's forces along with the rest of Washington's army continued to confront the British in Pennsylvania and New Jersey, but by late September, the British under Howe reached Germantown, Pennsylvania. Washington's army encamped in the Whitemarsh Valley, and Washington was determined to attack the British lines as soon as possible. After intelligence informed him that Howe had dispatched a considerable portion of his forces against American fortifications along the Delaware River, necessary for the British fleet to approach Philadelphia by water, Washington called a meeting of his general officers on September 28 to ask their opinion of an attack at Germantown. Wayne was one of a small group of officers who favored an immediate attack, while the other generals favored waiting until reinforcements arrived from the North.

Wayne expressed his opinion in a candid letter to his wifeon September 30: "DEAR Polly,–I thought that you had a mind far above being Depressed at a little unfavourable Circumstance— the Enemy's being in Possession of Phila is of no more Consequence than their being in possession of the City of New York or Boston—they may hold it for a time—but must leave it with Circumstances of shame and Disgrace before the Close of the Winter— Our Army is now in full health and spirits, and far stronger than it was at the Battle of the Brandywine— We are daily Receiving Reinforcements, and are now drawing near the Enemy—who will shortly pay dear for the little Advantages they have lately gained— Our Army to the northward under Gen'l Gates is Victorious—matters looked much more Gloomy in that Quarter four weeks ago— than they do at this time here—it is our turn next—and altho' appearances are a little Gloomy at present—yet they will be soon Dissipated and a more pleasing prospect take place– Give my kindest love and wishes to both Our Mothers and Sisters—tell them my sword will shortly point out the way to Victory peace and Happiness—kiss our little people for me— Remove my books and Valuable Writings some Distance from my own House—if not already done—this is but an Act of prudence—and not to be Considered as proceeding from any Other Motive."

The usually careful and prudent Washington took the advice of Wayne and the other generals who advocated an immediate attack. Thus, on October 3, Washington moved his 11,000-man army towards the enemy camp at Germantown. Wayne, with General Sullivan, comprised the right wing of the American forces, and Washington ordered them to march down Skippack Road towards the market-house in Germantown where the main body of the British forces were posted. Their advance was too rapid, and Wayne and Sullivan became trapped by the British forces when they were two miles ahead of the other American units.

Wayne would write his wife on October 6 a description of his forces' participation in the battle: "DEAR Polly,–On the 4th Instant at the dawn of day we attacked General Howe's Army at the upper end of Germantown— The Action soon became General—when we advanced on the Enemy with Charged Bayonets—they broke at first without waiting to Receive us —but soon formed again—when a heavy and well directed fire took place on each side— The Enemy again gave way—but being supported by the Grenadiers Returned to the Charge— Gen'l Sullivans Division & Conways Brigade were at this time Engaged to the Right or west of Germantown— whilst my Division had the Whole Right wing of the Enemy's Army to Encounter on the left or east of the Town—two thirds of our army being then too far to the east to afford us any Assistance. However the Unparalelled bravery of the troops surmounted every Difficulty, and the enemy retreated in the utmost Confusion— Our people Remembering the Action of the Night of the 20th of Sep'r near the Warren—pushed on with their Bayonets— and took Ample Vengeance for that Nights Work— Our Officers Exerted themselves to save many of the poor wretches who were Crying for Mercy—but to little purpose; the Rage and fury of the Soldiers were not to be Restrained for some time—at least not until great numbers of the Enemy fell by our Bayonets— the fog together with the smoke Occasioned by our Cannon, and Musketry —made it almost as dark as night—our people mistaking one Another for the Enemy frequently Exchanged several shots before they discovered their Error—we had now pushed the Enemy near three miles and were in possession of their whole Encampment when a large body of troops were Discovered Advancing on our left flank—which being taken for the Enemy we retreated. After Retreating for about two miles we found it was our own people— who were Originally Designed to Attack the Right Wing of the Enemy's Army— The fog and this mistake prevented us from following a victory that in all Human probability would have put an end to the American War— Gen'l Howe for a long time could not persuade himself that we had run from Victory—but the fog clearing up he ventured to follow us with all his Infantry, Grenadiers and Light Horse with some field pieces—I, at this time was in the Rear and finding Mr. Howe Determined to push us hard, drew up in Order of Battle—and waited his Approach— When he Advanced near we gave him a few Cannon shot with some Musketry—which caused him to break and Run with the utmost Confusion—this ended the Action of that day—which Continued without Intermission from daylight until near twelve O'Clock— I had forgotten to mention that my Roan Horse was killed under me within a few yards of the Enemy's front—and my left foot a little bruised by one of their Cannon shot—but not so much as to prevent me from walking—my poor horse Received one Musket Ball in the breast—and one in the flank at the same Instant that I had a slight touch on my left hand—which is scarcely worth mentioning—upon the Whole it was a Glorious day— Our men are in the highest Spirits—and I am Confident we shall give them a total Defeat the next Action; which is at no great Distance."

The Battle of Germantown was the last major engagement of the year, and in the wake of their victory at Germantown, the British occupied Philadelphia, forcing the Continental Congress to flee from the rebel capital to nearby York. By then, however, news of the Battle of Saratoga was heading for Europe. At Saratoga, Burgoyne had lost nearly 20% of his effective fighting during the battles at Saratoga, and after a few days his trapped army surrendered to the Americans.

Benjamin Franklin had been sent by Congress to France in December 1776 to secure a critically needed alliance, and he was an ideal choice for Enlightened France, which revered Franklin for his scientific accomplishments and his known reputation as a brilliant man. Franklin had also been a diplomat before the Revolution, spending several years in London on behalf of the colonies. However, the French refused to provide more than arms and money throughout 1777, until they learned in December 1777 about Saratoga and Burgoyne's surrender. With that news, French King Louis XVI entered into a formal military alliance with the United States, and in February 1778, France joined the war.

Meanwhile, as he looked for a place to establish his winter camp, Washington came across a small community known as Valley Forge. Located 20 miles northwest of Philadelphia, it seemed like an ideal location. There was plenty of empty land around the village in which his men could build shelters, and it was close enough to the British lines to keep an eye on their movements while being far enough away to keep them from attacking in force.

His army had repeatedly faced a lack of discipline and chronic disorganization, and Congress began to consider replacing Washington as commander after the fall of Philadelphia. General Gates, who had received the lion's share of the credit for Saratoga by marginalizing Benedict Arnold's role in the victory when he submitted his report to the Congress, was floated as an alternative, and Washington was understandably devastated. Making matters worse, the winter was unusually harsh, leading to an estimated 2,000 or so deaths in camp from diseases. Gouverneur Morris would later call the soldiers at Valley Forge a "skeleton of an army...in a naked, starving condition, out of health, out of spirits."

As for Wayne, he was constantly in favor of taking the offensive despite the Continental Army' condition and wrote as much even before the rebels had camped at Valley Forge. In a letter dated December 3, Washington wrote to Wayne, "SIR,--I wish to recall your attention to the important matter recommended to your Consideration some time ago—Namely the Adviseability of a Winter Campaign, & practicability of an Attempt upon Philad'a with the Aid of a Considerable body of Militia to be Assembled at an appointed time & place. Particular reasons urge me to request your Sentiments on this matter by the morning, & I shall expect to receive them accordingly in writing by that time."

Wayne wrote back to Washington the following day, "SIR,--I am not for a Winters Campaign in the Open field—the Distressed and Naked Situation of your Troops will not Admit of it. But if taking post at Wilmington & the Villages in its Vicinity— or Hutting at the Distance of about twenty Miles West of Phil'a by way of Quarters (which will not only support the Honor &

Reputation of your Army in the eyes of the Enemy and the States of Europe—but will give Confidence to America—and Cover this Country against the Horrid rapine and Devastation of a Wanton Enemy,) be Deemed making a Winters Campaign—I am then for it upon every principle of Honor—policy and justice. The probability of a Successful Attack upon Phil'a during the Winter depends so much on time, Season & a Variety of Other Circumstances—that the Calling out the Militia in General may not be Strictly Warrantable. Notwithstanding I wish to see a proper number Always hanging on the Skirts of the Enemy, sufficient to prevent any small parties from Committing Depredations—to save the Continental Troops from that fatigue—and should the Enemy move out in force—to give timely Notice thereof and to Assist in their Repulse—"

The equestrian statue of Wayne at Valley Forge

As Wayne's letter to Washington indicated, the conditions at Valley Forge were brutal that winter, and Wayne struggled while attending to the material needs of his men, trying to make sure they were adequately fed and clothed and recruiting replacements for soldiers lost to sickness or desertion. Since he was the commander of the Pennsylvania Line, he appealed to the government of the Commonwealth for the necessary supplies, and he did the same in appeals to the Continental Congress.

Perhaps not surprisingly, these were thankless and frustrating tasks. Wayne wrote the Secretary of War in February, "DEAR SIR,-On my Arrival in Camp I found the Division in a much worse Condition for the Want of Clothing and every Other matter than I expected— I am endeavouring to Remedy the Defects & hope soon to Restore Order, Introduce Discipline and Content—all which was much Wanting and desertion prevailing fast— I flatter myself that I have so much the Esteem and Confidence of my Troops—that Desertion will no longer take place— I am happy to Inform you that there is not a single Instance since my Return— I find the Enclosed Deficiency in Bayonets which I wish an Order for from the Board of War on Mr. William Henry at Lancaster— with directions to make them Eighteen Inches long in the blade together with an Equal Number of Scabbards and belts—I would also wish to exchange a Number of Rifles for Muskets and Bayonets— I don't like rifles—I would almost as soon face an Enemy with a good Musket and Bayonet without amunition—as with amunition without a Bayonet for altho' there are not many Instances of bloody bayonets yet I am Confident that one bayonet keeps off an Other— and for the Want of which the Chief of the Defeats we have met with ought in a great measure to be Attributed— the Enemy know ing the Defenseless State of our Riflemen rush on— they fly mix with or pass thro' the Other Troops and Communicate fears that is ever Incident to a retiring Corps— this Would not be the Case if the Riflemen had bayonets—but it would be still better if good muskets and bayonets were put into the hands of good Marksmen and Rifles entirely laid aside— for my own part I never Wish to see one—at least Without a Bayonet— I don't give this as Mere matter of Opinion or Speculation—but as matter of fact to the truth of Which I have more than Once been an Unhappy Witness— I am so fully Convinced of the bad policy of such arms that no reasoning will ever Eradicate that Conviction."

In May, Wayne wrote Pennsylvania's President Thomas Wharton, Jr., "DEAR SIR,-Enclosed is the Return of the 13 Regiments belonging to the State of Penns'a—you will Observe that they are very weak—the chief part of those Returned Sick at present—is for want of Clothing—being too naked to Appear on the parade— our Officers in Particular are in a most wretched Condition—I can't conceive the Reason why they are not supplied—I purchased Cloth &c at York last Jan'y Sufficient to Clothe great part of them—but have not heard what has been done with it I know it must be Distress ing to your Excellency to hear so many Repetitions of our wants—but whatever pain it may give you—I hourly experience much more from the Complaints and View of Worthy fellows who are Conscious of meriting some Attention and whose wretched Condition cannot be worse—they think any change must be for the better & too many have Risked Desertion—the Enclosed Order has lately put some stop to it—and had we

Clothing I am Confident that we should not have any more leave us where we now have twenty."

Wharton

Despite the difficulties, it was at Valley Forge that Washington truly forged his army. He introduced a more rigorous training program for his troops, sponsored by Prussian General Friedrich Wilhelm von Steuben, who had fought with Frederick the Great. Like the Marquis de Lafayette before him, von Steuben came to Washington's army via the recommendation of Benjamin Franklin, who hoped to use their appointments to curry political favor internationally. Despite speaking little English, von Steuben went about drafting a drill manual in French, and he personally presided over training drills and military parades. With the help of von Steuben, the Continental Army left Valley Forge in the spring of 1778 a more disciplined army than ever before, and the worst of Washington's failures were behind him.

Friedrich Wilhelm von Steuben

Pictures of a bust and statue of von Steuben at Valley Forge

Turning the Tide

Alonzo Chappel's engraving of Wayne

"Upon the whole it was a Glorious day-Our men are in the Spirits-and I am confident we shall give them a total defeat the next Action; which is at no great distance." – Anthony Wayne

France's entry into the war dramatically altered the strategic balance. The war became a global war, with much of Great Britain's possessions threatened. As a result, Great Britain was forced to spend more resources outside of the American theater. British strategy had to change to accommodate a global war; Great Britain had to protect its colonies in the West Indies, India and even guard against a potential French invasion of Ireland.

French participation also had an immediate effect on Great Britain's North American strategy. Prior to France's entry, Great Britain could move troops and supplies by sea with only minimal threat from American privateers. But France had a powerful navy that could threaten British troop movements, and attack British-held towns from the sea. Thus, the British shifted their strategy to trying to subdue the South.

After 1777, both sides became more active in the southern colonies. Realizing that the North could not be easily won, the British shifted attention to the South. The region had seen little action during the war, but the British thought the area was more loyal and would offer less resistance. Initially, it seemed the British plan might work. Though Loyalist allies were few, the British did find useful friends through the Cherokee Indians. Together, the British and Cherokee were able to control the coastal regions of North and South Carolina and Georgia by the end of 1779.

In June 1778, as the British were preparing to evacuate Philadelphia, Washington asked his generals their opinion about the upcoming campaign. Wayne wrote to Washington, "SIR,--I have Maturely Considered the Matters which your Excellency was pleased to lay before the Council of General Officers last evening—and am Clearly of Opinion that any attempt on the City of Philad'a with your present force when defended by the numbers of Troops that may be brought to act against you—will be Ineligible— But it is my wish & Opinion that you cause the sick in Camp and its vicinity to be Immediately Removed further into the Country—& that the whole of the Army be put in Motion the soonest possible for some of the ferries on the Delaware above Trent Town—so as to be Ready to act as soon as the Enemy's movem't shall be ascertained— If the North River should be found to be their Object—I am for passing the Delaware Immediately, Divesting the Army of every Article of Incumbrance—and then with the aid of the Jersey Militia take the first favorable Oppor tunity to make a Vigorous and serious attack upon the Enemy— but in Order to Complete your Victory or facilitate your Retreat (if the latter should be found necessary) I would wish that Gen'l Maxwell with his Brigade and a Body of the Militia might gain their Rear where his Action will be governed by your Motions—i.e. when the Attack is made by you—it shall be a signal for his onset which ought to be Rather a feint than Otherwise. Should your attack succeed it may be productive of the most happy Consequences—but should it prove unsuccessful the Enemy dare not nor can not pursue any great Distance, Otherwise their Baggage & provisions will be Endangered—surrounded as they will be by troops who know how to rally in case of a Misfortune and to Recoil upon their pursuers. I am the more anxious to take this Opportunity of striking them (in case they should take this route)—as I am Confident that the minds of the Soldiers of either Army will be much Influenc'd by our Movements— On the Enemy's part it will have the Appearance of a Retreat—on ours, that of Pursuit— We may Inculcate the Idea of Besieging Clinton—he will Apprehend it—and you will more than probably effect it—"

On June 28, 1778, forces led by Wayne attacked the British forces during the Battle of Monmouth. He recounted the battle in a letter to his wife written on July 1: "DEAR Polly,–On Sunday the 28th June our flying army came in view of the Enemy about Eight O'Clock in the Morning—when I was Ordered to Advance and Attack them with a few men—the Remainder of the Army under Gen'l Lee was to have supported me— We accordingly Advanced, and Received a Charge from the British horse and Infantry which we soon repulsed, however our Gen'l thought proper to retreat in place of Advancing—without our firing a single shot— The Enemy followed in force—which Rendered it very Difficult for the small force I had to gain the main body being Often hard pushed, and frequently surrounded— After falling back about a mile we met His Excellency—who was surprised at our Retreat, knowing that Officers as well as men were in high Spirits and wished for Nothing more than to be faced about and meet the British fire.— He Accordingly Ordered me to keep post where he met us with Stewarts & Livingstons Regiments and a Virginia Reg't then under my Command with two pieces of Artillery and to keep them in play until he had an opportunity of forming the Remainder of the Army and Restoring Order— We had but just taken post when the Enemy began their attack with Horse & foot & Artillery. The fire of their whole united force soon Obliged us after a Severe Conflict to give way—when a Most tremendous Cannonade Commenced on both sides, Continuing near four Hours without Ceasing— During this time every possible Exertion was made by His Excellency and the Other Generals to Spirit up the Troops and to prepare them for an Other tryal— The Enemy began to Advance again in a heavy Column against which I ordered some [torn out] Advanced with some of my Or [torn out] to meet them. The Action was Exceedingly warm and well Maintained on each Side for a Considerable time— At Length Victory Declared for us, the British Courage failed and was forced to give place to American Valour— We Encamped on the field of Battle where we found among the Dead and Wounded a Number of the first Officers of the British Army— We have taken a Great Many Prisoners—and their men are coming in to us by Hundreds of a Day— In this Affair we lost some brave Officers killed and Wounded. Every General & other officer (one excepted) did Everything that could be expected on this Great Occasion, but Pennsylvania shewed the Road to Victory— Adieu my Dear Polly. Send this to my poor old Mother & tell her that I am safe & Well. Kiss our Little People for me."

The following year, in July 1779, Washington awarded Wayne with the command of the Corps of Light Infantry. This new corps included two Connecticut regiments, one Virginia regiment, and Pennsylvanians regiments, organized into two brigades. Upon taking command of the force, Wayne addressed his new command: "The distinguished honor conferred upon every officer and soldier who has been drafted into this corps, by his Excellency General Washington, the credit of the States they respectively belong to, and their own reputations, will be such powerful motives for each man to distinguish himself, that the General cannot have the least doubt of a glorious victory. He hereby engages to reward the first man who enters the works…But should there be any soldier so lost to a feeling of honor as to attempt to retreat a single foot, or skulk in the face of danger, the officer next to him is immediately to put him to death, that he may no longer disgrace the name of a soldier, or the corps or the State to which he belongs."

Washington directed Wayne and his new Corps to engage in a hazardous operation: an attack on the British positions at Stony Point, one of two forts that guarded the approach to King's Ferry, New York. Stille described the fortification and the challenges facing any American assault: "The fort at Stony Point was built on a rocky promontory on the west side of the Hudson, about one hundred and fifty feet high. Three sides of this promon tory were surrounded by water, and on the fourth a swamp or morass, which was not passable at high tide, separated it from the land. It was guarded by three redoubts, and protected by a double abafis of logs, which extended across the peninsula. The cannon were so arranged as to enfilade any approach to the inner works supposed to be practicable. It had a garrison of about five hundred men, under the command of Colonel Johnston, who was regarded as a highly capable officer."

After a reconnaissance of the fortifications, Washington issued the following plan of attack to Wayne on July 10: "My ideas of the enterprise in contemplation are these : 'That it should be attempted by the Light Infantry only, which should march under cover of the night and with the utmost secrecy to the enemy's lines, securing every person they find to prevent discovery. 'Between one & two hundred chosen men & officers I conceive fully sufficient for the surprise, and apprehend that the approach should be along the water on the south side, crossing the beach and entering at the abattis. 'This party is to be preceded by a vanguard of prudent and determined men well commanded, who are to remove obstructions, secure the sentries, and drive in the guard. They are to advance (the whole of them) with fixed bayonets and muskets unloaded. The officers commanding them are to know precisely what batteries or particular parts of the line they are respectively to possess, so that confusion & the consequences of indecision may be avoided. 'These parties should be followed by the main body at a small distance for the purpose of support...Other parties may advance to the works by the way of the causeway & the River on the north if practicable as well for the purpose of distracting the enemy in their defence as to cut off their retreat...'If success should attend the enterprise measures should be taken to prevent the retreat of the garrison by water, or to annoy them as much as possible should they attempt it. The guns should be immediately turned against the shipping and Verplanck's point, and covered, if possible, from the enemy's fire. 'Secrecy is so much more essential to these kind of enterprises than numbers, that I should not think it advisable to employ any other than light troops. If a surprise takes place they are fully equal to the business, if it does not numbers will avail little."

On the night of July 15-16, 1779, Wayne led a nighttime bayonet attack with 1,500 men against the fortifications at Stony Point, capturing the fort and 550 prisoners in an assault that lasted all of 30 minutes. At 2:00 am on July 16, Wayne sent Washington a two sentence dispatch: "DEAR GEN'L,-The fort & garrison with Col. Johnston are ours. Our officers & men behaved like men who are determined to be free."

Wayne's assault won plaudits from around the colonies, and Washington issued a general order "congratulating the army on the success of the troops under General Wayne, who last night, with the Corps of Light Infantry, surprised and took the enemy's post at Stony Point with the whole garrison." On July 21, Washington wrote, "To the encomiums he [General Wayne] has deservedly bestowed upon the officers and men under his command, it gives me pleasure to add that his own conduct through the whole of this arduous enterprise merits the warmest approbation of Congress. He improved upon the plan recommended by me, and executed it in a manner that does signal honor to his judgment and bravery. In a critical moment of the assault he received a flesh wound in the head with a musket ball, but continued leading on his men with unshaken firmness."

The Continental Congress, on receiving word of the successful attack, immediately voted a unanimous resolution of thanks and directed the striking of a commemorative gold medal to be presented to Wayne. The Pennsylvania General Assembly approved the following resolution on October 10, 1779: "Resolved, That the thanks of this House be given to General Wayne and to the Officers & Soldiers of the Penn'a line for the courage & conduct displayed by them in the attack on Stony Point, the honor they have reflected on the State to which they belong, the Clemency they showed to those in their power in a Situation, when by the laws of war, & Stimulated by resentment occasioned by the remembrance of a former Massacre, they would have been justified in putting to death every one of the garrison, will transmit their names with honor to the latest posterity & show that true bravery & humanity are inseparable. Unanimously confirmed by the Supreme Executive Council."

It was after this battle that Wayne earned the nickname "Mad Anthony" for his tactical bravery and courage.

A depiction of Stony Point in Room S-128 of the U.S. Capitol

If the assault on Stony Point was the high point of Wayne's Revolutionary War career, the

Pennsylvania Line Mutiny was the lowest. The continual depreciation of the colonial currency, the lack of any pay at all, and the constant failures of the states and the Continental Congress to adequately supply the troops led members of the Pennsylvania Line to mutiny on January 1, 1781.

Wayne wrote the following account to Washington early in the morning the next day: "DEAR GENERAL,-It is with pain I now inform your Excellency of the general mutiny & defection which suddenly took place in the Penn'a line between 9 & 10 o'clock last evening— Every possible exertion was used by the officers to suppress it in its rise; but the torrent was too potent to be stemmed. Captain Bitting has fallen a victim to his zeal and duty, Captain Tolbert & Lieu tenant White are reported mortally wounded, a very considerable number of the field & other officers are much injured by strokes from muskets, bayonets & stones, nor have the rioters escaped with impunity— Many of their bodies lay under our horses' feet, and others will retain with existence the traces of our swords and espontoons. They finally moved from the ground about eleven o'clock last night, scouring the grand parade with round & grape shot from four field pieces, the troops advancing in solid column with fixed bayonets, producing a diffusive fire of musketry in front, flank & rear. During this horrid scene a few officers with myself were carried by the tide to the forks of the road at Mount Kemble, but placing ourselves on that leading to Elizabethtown, produced a conviction in the soldiery that they could not advance on that route but over our dead bodies. They fortunately turned towards Princeton. Colonels Butler & Stewart (to whose spirited exertions I am much indebted) will accompany me to Wealtown where the troops now are. We had our escapes last night— Should we not be equally fortunate to-day our friends will have this consolation, that we did not commit the honor of the United States or our own on this unfortunate occasion."

Over the next few weeks, the mutineers maintained a surprising order and respect for their commanding officers. At one point, a representative told Wayne, "We love you, we respect you, but you are a dead man if you fire. Do not mistake us: we are not going to the enemy; on the contrary, were they now to come out you would see us fight under your orders with as much resolution and alacrity as ever."

By January 29, thanks to the efforts of representatives from Pennsylvania, the mutiny was quelled and 1,250 members of the Line were discharged. On February 2, 1781, Washington wrote to Wayne, "I am satisfied, that everything was done on your part to produce the least possible evil from the unfortunate disturbance in your line, and that your influence has had a great share in preventing worse extremities— I felt for your Situation— Your anxieties & fatigues of mind amidst such a scene, I can easily conceive— I thank you sincerely for your exertions—" Wayne spent the next several months trying to get the Pennsylvania Line back up to full strength.

Colonial forces spent much of the spring of 1781 harassing Lord Cornwallis' British forces throughout the Carolinas, a campaign that culminated with the Battle of Guilford Courthouse. After driving Cornwallis out of North Carolina, the rebels pursued the British into Virginia, which led to the fateful Siege of Yorktown.

Washington and his men had stayed in the northern colonies throughout most of this time, but he decided in 1781 to coordinate movements south with the French toward Virginia. Washington's American forces and allied French troops joined together north of New York City and feinted a movement toward it to freeze the British in place before turning south to Virginia. Meanwhile, the French navy in the Western Hemisphere sailed to the Chesapeake Bay, blockading Yorktown. The French were able to maintain this blockade and defeated a British Navy effort to break it in the Battle of Chesapeake Bay.

In May 1781, Wayne brought the Pennsylvania Line south into Virginia to support the American forces in their operations against the British under Cornwallis. At the Battle of Green Springs on July 6, 1781, Wayne's small scouting force of 500 was ambushed by Cornwallis' forces, but they managed to hold out against superior numbers until reinforcements arrived and allowed Wayne to lead an orderly retreat. This proved to be the last major land battle in Virginia prior to the Siege of Yorktown.

When Washington arrived in Yorktown, the combined American and French forces totally surrounded Yorktown. After an extensive bombardment, the combined attack claimed the British defenses. With the French and American artillery shelling Yorktown from three sides, General Cornwallis was forced to surrender. Over 7,000 British officers and soldiers were captured, and the battle was the last major battle in North America, thus effectively ensuring the independence of the United States. Just thirteen days later, Cornwallis surrendered to Washington, handing him his sword. It is said that the British regimental band, recognizing the gravity of their defeat, played a popular tune of the time called "The World Turned Upside Down."

After the surrender of Cornwallis on October 19, 1781, Wayne wrote to Robert Morris, "The surrender of Lord Cornwallis with his Fleet & Army must have been announced in your city before this period It is an event of the utmost consequence & if properly Improved may be productive of a Glorious & happy peace; but if we suffer that unworthy torpor & supineness to seize us, which but too much pervaded the Councils of America after the Surrender of Gen'l Burgoyne, we may yet experience great Difficulties,—for believe me it was not to the exertions of America, that we owe the Reduction of this modern Hannibal, nor shall we always have it in our power to Command the aid of 37 sail of the Line & 8000 Auxiliary veterans— Our allies have learned, that on this Occasion, our regular troops were not more than equal to one half their Land force: and altho' our prowess was such as to establish our Character as Soldiers—our means & numbers were far inadequate to the Idea they had formed of American resources Yet the Resources of this Country are great & if Councils will call them forth we may produce a Conviction to the World that we deserve to be free—for my own part, I am such an Enthusiast for In dependence, that I would hesitate to enter heaven thro' the means of a secondary cause unless I had made the utmost exertions to merit it. The Pennsylvanians with some other troops have another field of glory in view—if successful you'l soon hear from us, till when & ever believe me yours."

Though Yorktown was the last major engagement of the Revolution, the war would not formally conclude until over a year later with the Treaty of Paris in 1783. Thus, after the surrender at Yorktown, Wayne traveled further south and engaged the Creek and Cherokee in Georgia, as they were allied with the British. He was able to successfully negotiate treaties of peace between the United States and both tribes, and for his efforts, Georgia awarded him a large rice plantation. He received promotion to the rank of Major General on October 10, 1783.

The Legion

Wayne spent the next several years after the war as a civilian, returning to Pennsylvania after his discharge from the Army. He was elected to the Pennsylvania Assembly from Chester County in 1784 and 1785, and he served as a delegate to the Pennsylvania Convention, organized in 1788 to ratify the proposed U.S. Constitution.

Despite staying in Philadelphia, Wayne attempted to run the plantation granted him by the state of Georgia, but it suffered many financial difficulties. At one point, the people of Georgia's 1st Congressional District elected him to the House of Representatives in 1790, but he lost his seat in 1791 when a House committee found that electoral fraud had been committed in the election. As it turned out, Wayne had not met the residential requirements to actually be Georgia's Congressman. Despite that conclusion, it was clear to all that Wayne had not been active in the fraud, nor was he even aware of the actions of the election officers.

The United States and Britain reached an impressively comprehensive peace in the Treaty of Paris. Among the important terms of the treaty, Britain recognized the colonies as free and relinquished territorial claims to them. The two sides then negotiated the boundaries that separated the United States from the British colonies in present-day Canada. Additionally, the British and Americans strove to share certain waters, including the Mississippi River and the fishing waters off Newfoundland. Finally, the two sides made mutual promises regarding paying debts and returning property that had been confiscated during the war, including slaves.

Still, the Treaty of Paris was not without its problems. Almost immediately, individual states in America rejected certain provisions and ignored them outright, a hallmark characteristic of American federalism that would lead to the Civil War 80 years later. Other problems included disputes along the boundary with Canada, and the fact that American access to the Mississippi River was blocked after the British and Spanish signed a separate treaty that left Spain in control of Florida. Some of these problems would fester heading into the 19th century, and eventually the British and Americans would go to war again in 1812.

The treaty had created a vast frontier for the fledgling nation, and any American settlers pushing west along it were bound to encounter hostile natives. It was partly for that reason that President Washington called on Wayne to lead American forces against the Western Confederacy of Indian Tribes in the Northwest Territory in 1792. Washington placed him in command of the newly formed Legion of the United States.

After traveling to Pittsburgh in June 1792, Wayne set about recruiting and organizing his forces, but he quickly had to deal with desertions and the jittery nerves of his own soldiers. He reported in August 1792, "Two nights since, upon a report that a large body of Indians were close in our front, I ordered the troops to form for action, and rode along the line to inspire them with confidence, and gave a charge to those in the redoubts, which I had recently thrown up in our front and right flank, to maintain their post at any expense of blood until I could gain the enemy's rear with the dragoons; but such is the defect of the human heart, that from excess of cowardice one third of the sentries deserted from their stations so as to leave the most accessible places unguarded."

Wayne decided that a long, rigorous course of training his new recruits would be necessary before he led them into battle, so he set up a training camp outside Pittsburgh which he called Legionville. In doing so, Wayne established the U.S. Military's first basic training facility.

There, his force stayed through the fall and winter, gaining the training and discipline necessary to become an effective fighting force. By the close of March 1793, he was able to report, "The progress that the troops have made both in manoeuvring and as marksmen astonished the savages on St. Patrick's day; and I am happy to inform you that the sons of that Saint were perfectly sober and orderly, being out of the reach of whiskey, which BANEFUL POISON is prohibited from entering this camp except as the component part of a ration, or a little for fatigue duty or on some extraordinary occasion."

A depiction of Wayne with the Legion

A modern picture of the site of Legionville

A marker at the site

In May 1793, he moved his camp to Fort Washington, the present site of Cincinnati, where he received continual orders from the Secretary of War to avoid taking offensive operations against the natives while negotiations were going on. Naturally, Wayne chafed under the restraints, writing to the Secretary of War in October, "I will advance to-morrow with the force I have in order to take up a position in front of Fort Jefferson, so as to keep the enemy in check by exciting a jealousy and apprehension for the safety of their women and children, until some favorable circumstance or opportunity may present to strike with effect. I pray you not to permit present appearances to cause too much anxiety either in the mind of the President or yourself on account of this army. Knowing the critical situation of our infant nation, and feeling for the honor and reputation of the government (which I will support with my latest breath), you may rest assured that I will not commit the Legion unnecessarily. Unless more powerfully supported than I have reason to expect, I will content myself with taking a strong position in advance of Fort Jefferson, and by exerting every power endeavor to protect the frontier and secure the posts and the army during the winter, or until I am favored with your further orders."

On June 30, 1794, a small body of Wayne's forces was attacked near Fort Recovery, and that attack was followed by an assault on the fort, but the attack was repulsed. A few days later,

Wayne's forces were joined by a group of Kentucky volunteers.

From Greeneville, he advanced 70 miles into Indian country and constructed a fort at the conjunction of Le Glaize and Miami Rivers, which he called Fort Defiance. He sent the native tribes another overture for peace, one they spurned, and this led to one of the most consequential battles against Native Americans in history.

A picture of Wayne and the Legion advancing along the Maumee River

That battle, fought on August 20, 1794, is now known as the Battle of Fallen Timbers, and though there weren't many casualties on either side, it resulted in a decisive American victory that essentially pushed the British out of the Northwest Territory altogether, a crucial step for the country's westward expansion.

On August 28, 1794, Wayne described the action in a letter written to the Secretary of War: "SIR,--It is with infinite pleasure that I now announce to you the brilliant success of the Federal Army under my command in a general action with the combined force of the hostile Indians and a considerable number of the volunteers & militia of Detroit (Canadians) on the 20th inst on the banks of the Miamis in the Vicinity of the British post and garrison at the foot of the rapids....From every account the enemy amounted to 2000 combatants, and the troops actually engaged against them were short of 9oo. This horde of savages with their allies abandoned themselves to flight, and dispersed with terror and dismay leaving our victorious army in full & quiet possession of the field of battle which terminated under the influence of the guns of the British garrison, as you will perceive by the enclosed correspondence between Major Campbell, the commandant, & myself upon the occasion. The bravery & conduct of every officer belonging to the army from the Generals down to the Ensigns merit my highest approbation."

   As a result of the battle, the tribes in the Northwest Territory were forced to negotiate with the United States, and in August 1795, the Treaty of Greenville ceded to the United States a vast tract of territory west of the Ohio River and north to Detroit.

A painting of the treaty negotiations

An early 20th century commemorative stamp for Wayne and the Battle of Fallen Timbers

Wayne continued to lead the Legion to secure the frontier, but his health began to decline in the years after the Battle of Fallen Timbers. He was suffering from gout, a condition that had actually disabled him around the time of that decisive battle, and on November 17, 1796, as he sailed from Detroit for Presqu'isle (the present site of Erie, Pennsylvania), he had a serious attack of gout. The disease reached his stomach, leaving Wayne in agony for several weeks before he finally died on December 15, 1796. He was buried in Fort Presque Isle, and in 1809, his son Isaac had his body disinterred and moved to the family plot in the graveyard of St. David's Episcopal Church in Wayne, Pennsylvania.

The Society of the Cincinnati, founded by Washington and other Revolutionary War veterans in the wake of winning the country's independence, erected a monument over Wayne's grave with the following inscription: "MAJOR GENERAL ANTHONY WAYNE was born at

Waynesborough In Chester County State of Pennsylvania A.D. 1745. After a life of Honor & Usefulness He died in December 1796, At a military post On the shores of Lake Erie Commander-in-chief of the Army of The United States. His military achievements Are consecrated In the history of his country And in The hearts of his countrymen. His Remains Are Here Deposited. In honor of the distinguished Military Services of MAJOR-GENERAL ANTHoNY WAYNE And as an affectionate tribute of respect to his Memory This Stone was erected by his Companions In Arms, The Pennsylvania State Society of The Cincinnati, July 4th A.D. 1809, Thirty fourth anniversary of The Independence of the United States, An event which constitutes the most Appropriate Eulogium of an American Soldier and Patriot.

A picture of Wayne's grave

Online Resources

Other Revolutionary Era titles by Charles River Editors

Further Reading

Allen, William B. (1872). A History of Kentucky: Embracing Gleanings, Reminiscences, Antiquities, Natural Curiosities, Statistics, and Biographical Sketches of Pioneers, Soldiers, Jurists, Lawyers, Statesmen, Divines, Mechanics, Farmers, Merchants, and Other Leading Men, of All Occupations and Pursuits. Bradley & Gilbert. pp. 46–47. Retrieved November 10, 2008.

Boatner, Mark M., III (1994). Encyclopedia of the American Revolution. Mechanicsburg, Pa.: Stackpole Books. ISBN 0-8117-0578-1.

Carter, Harvey Lewis (1987). The Life and Times of Little Turtle: First Sagamore of the Wabash. Urbana: University of Illinois Press. ISBN 0-252-01318-2.

Dubin, Michael J (1998). United States Congressional Elections, 1788–1997: The Official Results of the Elections of the 1st through 105th Congresses. Jefferson, NC: McFarland and Company. ISBN 0-7864-0283-0.

Knopf, Richard C. (ed) (1960). Anthony Wayne: A Name in Arms. Pittsburgh: University of Pittsburgh Press.

Labaree, Leonard W. (ed.) (1968). The Papers of Benjamin Franklin, Vol. 12. Philadelphia: American Philosophical Society.

Lancaster, Bruce (1971). The American Revolution. New York: American Heritage Books. ISBN 0-618-12739-9.

Nelson, Paul David (1985). Anthony Wayne. Soldier of the Early Republic. Bloomington, Indiana: Indiana University Press. ISBN 0-253-30751-1.

Pleasants, Henry; Delaware County Historical Society (1907). History of Old St. David's Church Radnor, Delaware County, Pennsylvania. John C Winston Co. p. 206.

Free Books by Charles River Editors

We have brand new titles available for free most days of the week. To see which of our titles are currently free, <u>click on this link</u>.

Discounted Books by Charles River Editors

We have titles at a discount price of just 99 cents everyday. To see which of our titles are currently 99 cents, click on this link.

www.ingramcontent.com/pod-product-compliance
Lightning Source LLC
Chambersburg PA
CBHW080851160726
47999CB00009B/3077